SCHOOL DAYS

Written by: Heddrick M. McBride

Illustrated by: Alex Baranov

Edited by: Tilea Coleman

School Days

ISBN-10:0615709230
ISBN-13:978-0615709239

THE COOKING CLASS

One moment this year that will always last.

We all signed up for a cooking class.

First thing we learned about was kitchen safety.

We should take our time while cooking and not be hasty.

We learned to crack eggs without leaving the shells.

Miguel cracked his tooth and loudly he yelled.

We spent the next two days reading recipes.

If anyone was allergic to a dish, we would clearly see.

Next we learned how to properly open cans.

Donald did it wrong, and he hurt his hands.

Then we learned how to measure sugar and salt.

If your food tasted bad, then it was probably your fault.

Our teacher quickly directed us to the microwave.

It was safer than fire, and much time it would save.

We peeled potatoes and rolled out cookie dough.

They both could be done either fast or slow

The final lesson we had was how to set the table.

It could turn out beautiful if you are able.

Those two weeks were really a blast.

We learned so much in cooking class.

What a great way to end the school year.

We had a field day that was full of cheer.

Some events took place outside, and the rest were in the gym.

Trophies would be given out to the team that wins.

We were divided into two teams by the colors of our jerseys.

The crowd will cheer loudly for the team that is most worthy.

The Green Team was Donald, Carmen, Hector, and Little Mike.

They looked like a crew that any coach would like.

Sky, Miguel, Vanessa, and Shawn had shirts that were yellow.

When you saw them in action, all you can do is say HELLO!

The competition was close, as both teams were full of winners.

Yellow Jackets were faster, but the Green Machine had better swimmers.

Carmen won the hula hoop because she lasted longest.

Shawn won the chicken throw, and proved he was the strongest.

Hector beat Miguel in overtime to become the ping pong champ.

Then Miguel beat him in a rope climb; a skill that he learned at camp.

Shawn knocked down 10 soda bottles to win the Bowling Bash.

Donald won the free throw contest because his jump shot was cash.

Vanessa won at miniature golf and the Frisbee toss.

She went through both events without a loss.

During the game of tug of war, both teams let go of the rope.

There was no winner, but now they both needed some soap.

The score was tied and all that was left was the balance beam.

The Green Machine had to use the weakest link of their team.

Little Mike hadn't competed in anything all day.

It was against the rules to treat your teammate this way.

Yellow Team used Jada, and she lasted 30 seconds.

It would be tough for anyone to beat this new record.

Who thought Little Mike would win? The final vote was zero.

He lasted 40 seconds, and became our *Field Day Hero*!

One of the best days of the year had to be our School Trip.

Before we could go our parents had to sign a permission slip.

I was running late that morning, so to school I had to rush.

There it was as plain as day; the big yellow bus.

All my friends were on the bus; seated in the back.

We sat back there so that we could crack jokes and eat snacks.

About ten times our teacher had to tell us to be quiet.

We were so excited that we couldn't even if we tried it.

In front of the Museum was a huge fountain with running water.

Before we could go inside, we had to stand in size order.

We made sure not to run or lean against the glass.

No question was a dumb one, so anything we could ask.

We saw some great things, like the butterfly collection.

We also saw colorful flies while visiting that section.

There was also the exhibit full of dinosaur bones.

I would be scared to death if they showed up at my home.

We sat on a space shuttle and walked through Tornado Alley.

Lunch time was next, so to the lunch room went our rally.

We exchanged lunches, and that provided me with a laugh.

My friend made peanut butter and pickles, and offered me half.

When it was time to go, we bought souvenirs to go home with.

I had a great time on my first school trip.

What an exciting day we just had a Science Fair.

You could tell that all of the projects were done with great care.

Mike made a big volcano, which was pretty neat.

When it erupted, spaghetti sauce landed all over his feet.

Susie used dry ice to freeze some bubbles.

She finished this exhibit without causing any trouble.

Alex had a dirty farm full of bugs and ants.

Lisa showed us how hearing music can affect plants.

Before Ken's Solar System fell, it stood nice and tall.

The Earth was too heavy, because he used a tennis ball.

I used ammonia to make liquid magnets.

It was nice, but I don't think that the judge could understand it.

We had to cover our noses for the experiment about mold.

Donald used some cheese and bread that was very old.

Everyone did well and we all received ribbons.

For every exhibit a round of applause was given.

Jada won the contest because her invention was nice.

She used baking soda and vinegar to create hot ice.

We all used our imaginations; that was very clear.

I'll never forget my first Science Fair.

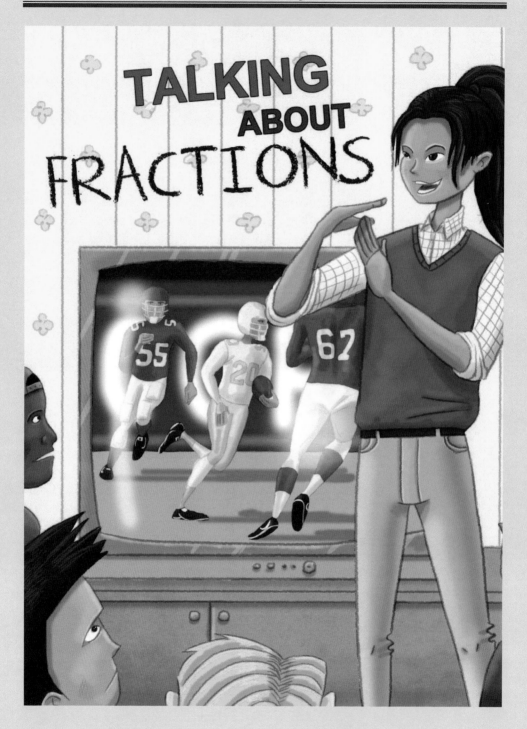

Studying with friends is cool, if everyone gives their best.

We all met at my house to study for a math test.

Friends, we don't need a book to talk about fractions.

We use them everyday in most of our actions.

Fractions are pieces that are taken from the whole.

Just like the half of your sandwich that my dog stole.

Fractions can also be seen while we are watching sports.

Every quarter of a football game equals one-fourth.

The numerator is the number that goes on top of everything.

This is the amount that is taken from the whole object you may bring.

So, if you see three books on the chair and you put away two.

Two is the numerator, and one book will be left when you're through.

The denominator is the number that goes underneath.

That is the total amount of books that you first found on the seat.

So, on the seat were three books that are filled with words.

Each book by itself represents one third.

After we finished studying my Mom gave us our prizes.

She gave us a pizza that was cut into five equal slices.

Learning about fractions is a very special gift.

But it didn't taste as good as that one-fifth!

Visit www.mcbridestories.com for more titles.

Made in the USA
Charleston, SC
07 April 2013